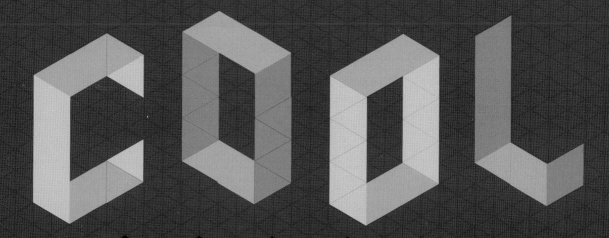

COOL

STRING ART

CREATIVE ACTIVITIES THAT MAKE MATH & SCIENCE FUN FOR KIDS!

A Division of ABDO
ABDO
Publishing Company

ANDERS HANSON AND ELISSA MANN

VISIT US AT WWW.ABDOPUBLISHING.COM

Published by ABDO Publishing Company, a division of ABDO, P.O. Box 398166, Minneapolis, Minnesota 55439. Copyright ® 2014 by Abdo Consulting Group, Inc. International copyrights reserved in all countries. No part of this book may be reproduced in any form without written permission from the publisher. Checkerboard Library™ is a trademark and logo of ABDO Publishing Company.

Printed in the United States of America, North Mankato, Minnesota
062013
112013

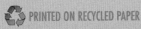 PRINTED ON RECYCLED PAPER

Design and Production: Anders Hanson, Mighty Media, Inc.
Series Editor: Liz Salzmann
Photo Credits: Anders Hanson, Shutterstock

LIBRARY OF CONGRESS CATALOGING-IN-PUBLICATION DATA

Hanson, Anders, 1980-
Cool string art : creative activities that make math & science fun for kids! / Anders Hanson and Elissa Mann.
    pages cm. -- (Cool art with math & science)
Includes index.
 ISBN 978-1-61783-824-8
1. Geometry--Juvenile literature. 2. Astronomy--Juvenile literature. 3. Mathematical recreations--Juvenile literature. 4. Scientific recreations--Juvenile literature. 5. String craft--Juvenile literature. 6. Creative activities and seat work--Juvenile literature. I. Mann, Elissa, 1990- II. Title.
 QA445.5.H364 2013
 516'.154--dc23
                       2013001895

CONTENTS

4 COOL STRING ART
LINES IN SPACE

6 A PERFECT FIT
REGULAR POLYGONS AND CIRCLES

8 PROJECT 1
STRING ART POLYGONS

12 WRITING
LETTERS AND LINES

14 PROJECT 2
STRING ART LETTER

18 ASTRONOMY
THE OLDEST SCIENCE

20 PROJECT 3
STRING ART CONSTELLATION

24 PLANETS
THE GREAT EIGHT

26 PROJECT 4
STRING ART PLANETS

30 MATH TERMS

31 GLOSSARY

31 WEB SITES

32 INDEX

COOL

STRING ART

LINES IN SPACE

Making string art is a fun way to play with lines. This book will show you how to make string art. You'll learn cool stuff about geometry, history, and astronomy too!

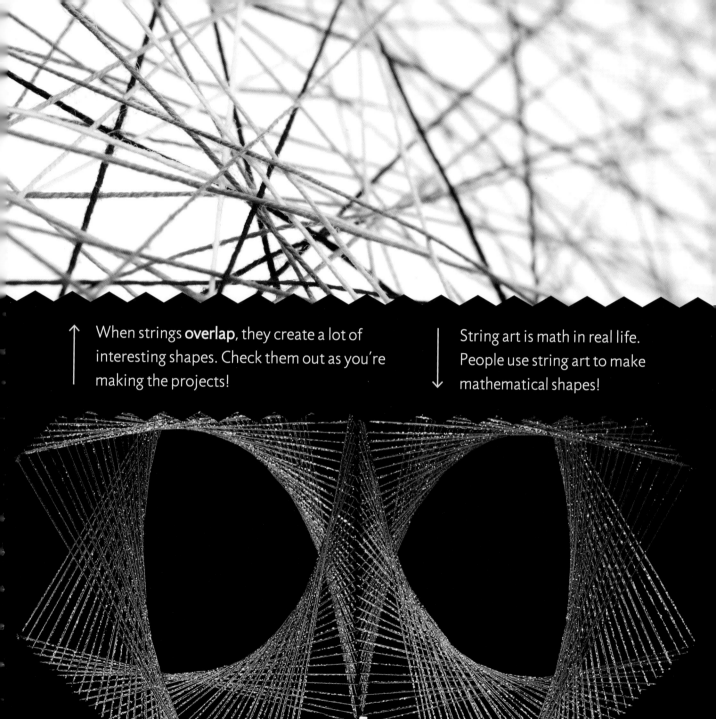

When strings **overlap**, they create a lot of interesting shapes. Check them out as you're making the projects!

String art is math in real life. People use string art to make mathematical shapes!

A PERFECT FIT
REGULAR POLYGONS AND CIRCLES

A polygon is a shape with straight sides. In regular polygons, such as squares, the sides are all the same length. The angles of a regular polygon are equal. Any regular polygon will fit perfectly inside a circle. All of the vertices will lie on the circle.

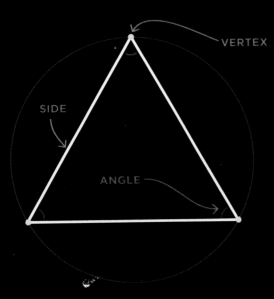

VERTEX

SIDE

ANGLE

EQUILATERAL TRIANGLE
(3 SIDES, 3 VERTICES, 60-DEGREE ANGLES)

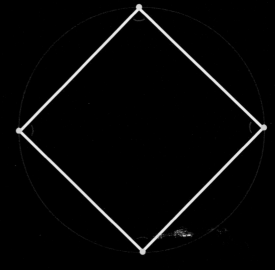

SQUARE
(4 SIDES, 4 VERTICES, 90-DEGREE ANGLES)

As the number of sides increases, the number of angles does too. The angles become wider. The points get closer to each other. The polygon begins to look more and more like a circle!

REGULAR HEXAGON
(6 SIDES, 6 VERTICES, 120-DEGREE ANGLES)

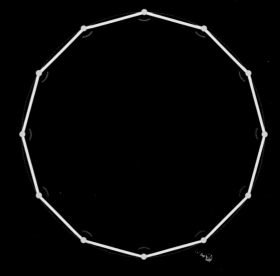

REGULAR DODECAGON
(12 SIDES, 12 VERTICES, 150-DEGREE ANGLES)

8

PROJECT

1

STRING ART POLYGONS

◆◆◆◆◆◆◆

STUFF YOU'LL NEED

- COMPASS WITH PENCIL
- THUMBTACKS
- CORKBOARD
- STRING
- SCISSORS
- PAPER

TERMS

- POLYGON
- CIRCLE
- INTERSECT
- TRIANGLE
- SQUARE
- HEXAGON
- DODECAGRAM
- GEOMETRIC

Use a circle to create geometric string art shapes. You can create many different polygons. Try them all!

The photo on the left shows part of a complete graph. Each point in the circle is connected to every other point. How many polygons in the photo can you name?

MAKE THE TEMPLATE

1   Use the compass to draw a large circle.

2   Set the compass to half of its previous length. Place the compass point anywhere on the circle. Draw a half circle.

3   Put the compass point where the half circle and the large circle intersect. Draw another half circle. Repeat until no more half circles can be drawn.

4   Cut out the large circle. Set it on the corkboard. **Insert** a tack into each point where a half circle intersects with the large circle. Erase the pencil lines. Number the tacks clockwise, from 1 to 12.

THE TRIANGLE

5   Tie the string around tack 1. Wrap the string around the outside of tacks 5, 9, and 1.

THE SQUARE

▶ **6** Tie the string around tack 1. Wrap the string around the outside of tacks 4, 7, 10, and 1.

THE HEXAGON

▶ **7** Tie the string around tack 1. Wrap the string around the outside of tacks 3, 5, 7, 9, 11, and 1.

THE DODECAGRAM

▶ **8** Tie the string around tack 1. Wrap the string around the outside of tacks 6, 11, 4, 9, 2, 7, 12, 5, 10, 3, 8, and 1.

THE COMPLETE GRAPH

9 A complete graph connects all 12 points together. Tie the string around tack 1. Go in any order to connect the tacks. Make sure each tack is connected to all of the other tacks.

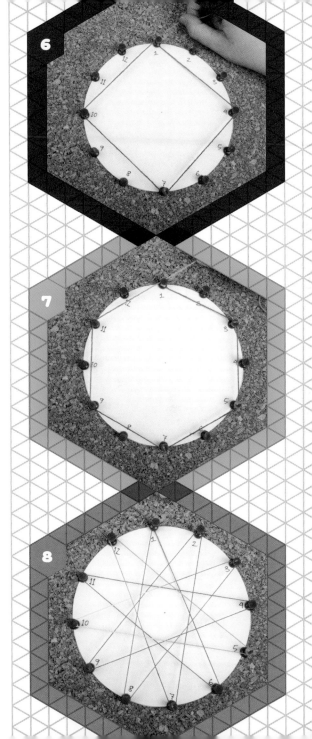

WRITING

LETTERS AND LINES

Writing is a common use for lines on paper. Letters and words are just lines bent into different shapes. Writing did not always look like it does today. It changed over time.

The first writing was invented in Sumeria around 3200 B.C. The Sumerians pressed the tips of reeds into clay **tablets**. Writing started to look more like it does now in 900 B.C. That is when the Phoenician **alphabet** was widely used.

PHOENICIAN LETTERS	✠	◁	∧	◿	∃	Y		⊟	⁓	
GREEK LETTERS	◁	8	◁	△	∃	∃		⊟	≀	
LATIN LETTERS	A	B	C	D	E	F	G	H	I	

Around 800 B.C. the Greeks developed their alphabet. They borrowed a lot from the Phoenicians. The Greek language still uses the Greek alphabet. The Romans created the Latin alphabet in 600 B.C. They borrowed a lot from the Greeks. Today, most Western languages, including English, use the Latin alphabet.

Compare the shapes from the Phoenician alphabet, the Greek alphabet, and the Latin alphabet. Find the similarities!

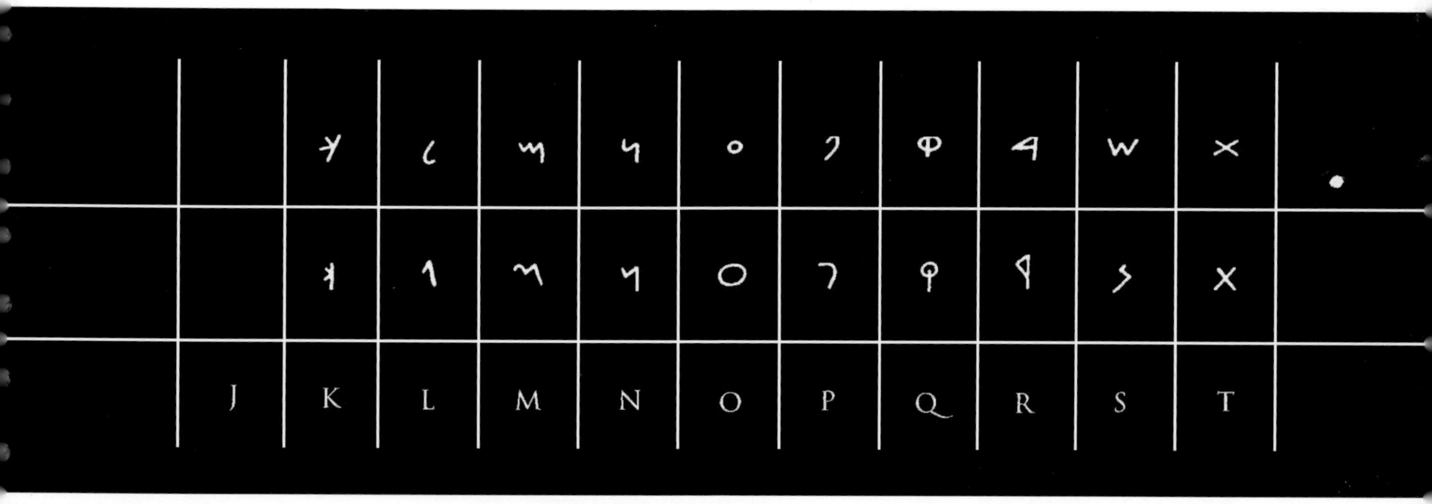

	ⴾ	�païç	ᵐ	ᴎ	o	ᒃ	φ	◁	w	×	
	ⴿ	ᴧ	ᵐ	ᴎ	O	ᒃ	φ	ᴅ	ᒃ	X	
J	K	L	M	N	O	P	Q	R	S	T	

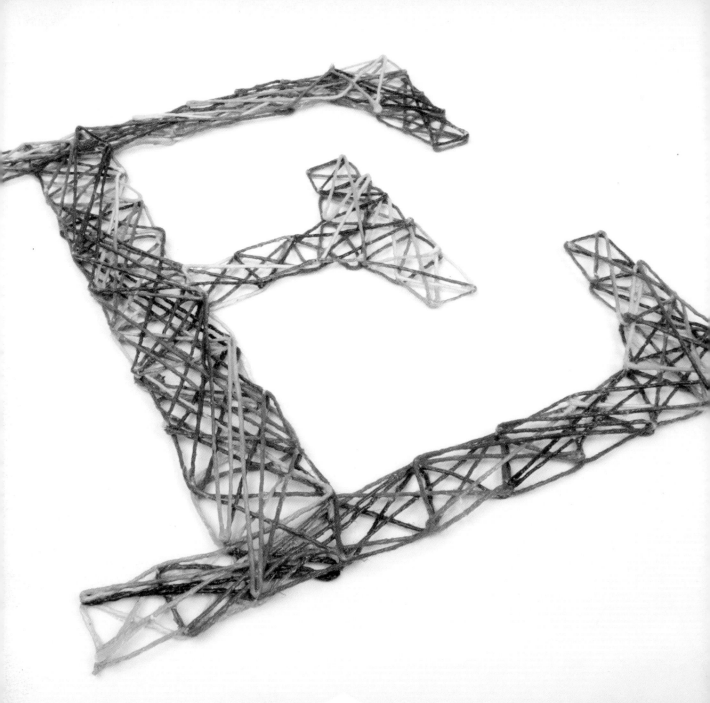

PROJECT 2

STRING ART LETTER

STUFF YOU'LL NEED

- CORKBOARD
- WAXED PAPER
- PAPER
- SCISSORS
- TAPE
- COLORED STRING
- PUSH PINS
- GLUE
- FOAM BRUSH

TERMS

- ALPHABET
- LETTER

The Latin alphabet has its roots in the Phoenician alphabet. The letters changed over time. Many letters still look similar.

Today, the most frequently used letter in the English language is *E*. The Latin *E* looks like a letter in the Phoenician alphabet. Can you figure out which one?

Try making your own letter in this project!

HOW TO MAKE IT

1   Cover the corkboard with a sheet of waxed paper.

2   Draw the letter you are using on a piece of paper. Or you can print the letter out from a computer. Make the letter big enough to fill most of the corkboard. Cut out the letter.

3   Place the letter cutout on the waxed paper. Tape it in place.

4   **Insert** pushpins around the edges of the letter. Space the pins equally. Don't put them through the letter.

5   Remove the letter cutout.

6 Tie one end of string around a pin. Wrap the string a couple of times around the nearby pushpins. Then begin wrapping around new pins. Cross the string back and forth inside the letter. Keep wrapping until the entire letter shape is filled.

7 Tie the end of the string to a pin. Cut off the excess.

8 Use a foam brush to apply glue to the string. Let the glue dry.

9 Carefully remove the pins. Flip the letter over.

10 Apply a coat of glue to the back of the letter. Let the glue dry.

ASTRONOMY
THE OLDEST SCIENCE

Astronomy is the study of stars, planets, and other objects in space. It is the oldest science. Throughout history, astronomers used stars to learn about the world.

Astronomers have grouped some stars into constellations. The first constellations were identified nearly 2,000 years ago by Claudius Ptolemy. He was a Greek astronomer.

There are now 88 constellations recognized by the International Astronomical Union.

Constellations were used to navigate. They were also used to form calendars and keep track of time.

Many constellations have **memorable** geometric shapes and lines. One of the most well-known constellations is Ursa Major.

Ursa Major means *Big Bear*.

The seven brightest stars of Ursa Major have many names. In the United States and Canada they are called the Big Dipper. In England and Ireland they are called the Plough.

Ursa Major
"The Big Dipper"

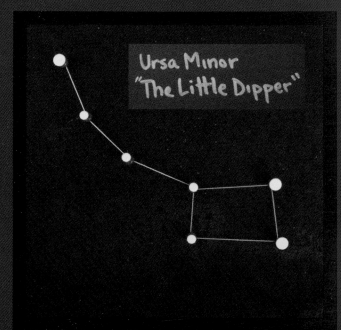

Ursa Minor
"The Little Dipper"

Orion
"The Hunter"

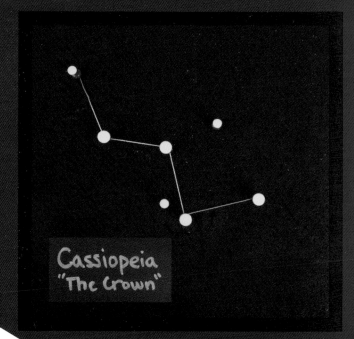

Cassiopeia
"The Crown"

PROJECT 3

STRING ART CONSTELLATION

◆◆◆◆◆◆◆

▶ STUFF YOU'LL NEED

- CORKBOARD
- BLACK ACRYLIC PAINT
- FOAM BRUSH
- GLOW-IN-THE-DARK STICKERS
- THUMB TACKS
- SCISSORS
- STRING
- PAPER
- PEN OR MARKER

▶ TERMS

- STAR
- CONSTELLATION

B ecome an astronomer in your own room! Take the stars inside with you.

Use glow-in-the-dark stickers to make your favorite constellations. Display them on your wall or ceiling. At night, you'll be stargazing inside!

HOW TO MAKE IT

1. Paint the corkboard black. Let the paint dry.

2. Pick a constellation to make. Choose a constellation on page 20, or look one up online.

3. Count out the same number of tacks as stars in the constellation. Put a glow-in-the-dark sticker on the top of each tack.

4. Use the tacks to create the constellation on the corkboard.

5 Tie the string around a tack. Wrap the string around every tack in the constellation. Pull the string tight to form lines connecting the stars. Go around each tack only once.

6 Tie the string to the last tack. Cut off any excess string.

7 Write the name of the constellation on a piece of paper. Glue it to the corkboard.

8 Have an adult help hang your constellation on a wall or ceiling. Turn out the lights. Watch it glow!

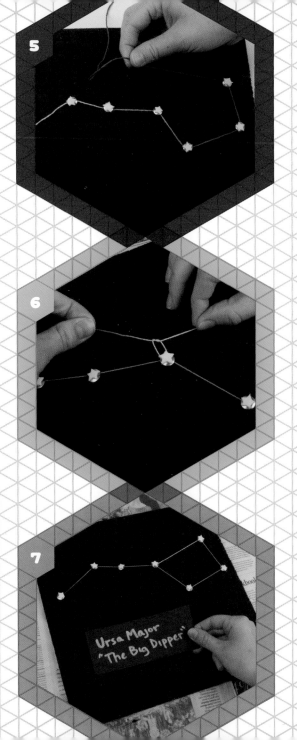

PLANETS
THE GREAT EIGHT

In ancient times, people thought the planets were gods. The Greeks and Romans named the planets after their gods. We still use most of those names today! The eight planets are Mercury, Venus, Earth, Mars, Jupiter, Saturn, Uranus, and Neptune.

THE SUN

MERCURY

VENUS

EARTH

MARS

JUPITER

People once thought the sun and planets revolved around Earth. They believed Earth was the center of the universe. That is why Earth was not named after a god. Instead, its name comes from the Old High German word *Erda*. It means *ground*.

SATURN

NEPTUNE

URANUS

This image shows the relative sizes of the planets. The distance between the planets has been shortened to show them all. They are much further apart!

PROJECT

4

STRING ART PLANETS

◆◆◆◆◆◆◆◆

The solar system is huge! Neptune is 2.8 billion miles (4.5 billion km) away from the sun.

Shrink the solar system down to size. Make these string art planets!

STUFF YOU'LL NEED

- NEWSPAPER
- PLASTIC SHEET
- ROPE
- STRING
- BALLOONS
- GLUE
- WATER
- CORNSTARCH
- PAPER BOWL
- THUMB TACK
- PAINTBRUSH
- PAINT
- 2 CHAIRS
- CLOTHESPINS
- POSTER BOARD

TERMS

- PLANET

HOW TO MAKE IT

1 Cover a table with newspaper. Spread the plastic sheet on the floor for a drying area. Place two chairs on the plastic sheet. They should be about 1 foot (30 cm) apart. Tie the rope between the chairs.

2 Blow up the balloons. Make two large balloons, two medium balloons, and four small balloons. The large balloons will be Jupiter and Saturn. The medium balloons will be Uranus and Neptune. The small balloons will be Mercury, Venus, Earth, and Mars.

3 Put ¼ cup (59 ml) glue and 1 cup (236 ml) cornstarch in a bowl. Slowly mix in ½ cup (118 ml) hot water.

4 Unroll the string. Soak the string in the glue mixture.

5 Tie one end of the string around the knot of a balloon.

6 Wrap the string around the balloon. **Overlap** the string many times.

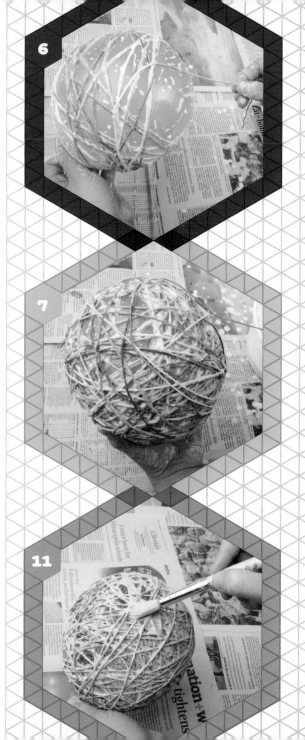

7 Soak more string in the glue if needed. Keep wrapping the balloon until it is covered with string.

8 Tie the string to the knot of the balloon. Cut off the excess. Hang the balloon from the rope with a **clothespin**.

9 Repeat steps 3–8 with the other seven balloons. Let them dry overnight.

10 Once the string is dry, pop the balloons with a thumb tack. Carefully remove the balloons from inside the balls.

11 Paint each ball like a planet in the solar system. To include Saturn's rings, cut out a ring of poster board that fits tightly around the planet. Paint it to match Saturn's colors.

12 Have an adult help hang the planets from the ceiling.

MATH TERMS

ALPHABET - a set of symbols that represent sounds.

CIRCLE - a curved line in which every point on the line is the same distance from the center.

CONSTELLATION - one of the 88 named groups of stars recognized by the International Astronomical Union.

DODECAGRAM - a twelve-pointed polygon shaped like a star.

GEOMETRIC - made up of straight lines, circles, and other shapes.

GRAPH - a chart or illustration that shows information about the amount of something.

HEXAGON - a shape with six straight sides and six angles.

INTERSECT - to meet and cross at a point.

LETTER - a symbol that represents a sound.

PLANET - one of the objects in space that go around the sun, such as Earth and Mars.

POLYGON - a two-dimensional shape with any number of sides and angles.

SQUARE - a shape with four straight, equal sides and four equal angles.

STAR - a ball of burning gas that looks like a point of light in the night sky.

TRIANGLE - a shape with three straight sides.

GLOSSARY

CLOTHESPIN - a clamp used to fasten laundry to a clothesline.

INSERT - to stick something into something else.

MEMORABLE - worth remembering, or easy to remember.

OVERLAP - to lie partly on top of something.

TABLET - a flat piece of stone or clay that words and symbols can be carved into.

WEB SITES

To learn more about math and science, visit ABDO Publishing Company on the World Wide Web at www.abdopublishing.com. Web sites about creative ways for kids to experience math and science are featured on our Book Links page. These links are routinely monitored and updated to provide the most current information available.

INDEX

A

Alphabets/Letters
  history of, 12–13
  project with, 15–17
Astronomy
  elements of, 18–19, 24–25
  projects with, 21–23, 27–29

C

Circles, 6, 7
Complete graphs, 8–9, 11
Constellations
  project with, 21–23
  study of, 18–19

D

Dodecagrams, 11

G

Geometry
  elements of, 6–7
  projects with, 9–11
Greek alphabet/ letters, 12–13

H

Hexagons, 11

L

Latin alphabet/ letters, 12–13, 15

P

Phoenician alphabet/ letters, 12–13, 15
Planets
  project with, 27–29
  study of, 24–25
Polygons
  definition of, 6
  project with, 9–11
  qualities of, 6–7
Ptolemy, Claudius, 18

R

Regular polygons, 6

S

Squares, 6, 11
String art
  projects with, 9–11, 15–17, 21–23, 27–29
  qualities of, 4–5
  template for, 10

T

Templates, 10
Triangles, 6, 10

W

Web sites, about math and science, 31
Writing
  history of, 12–13
  project with, 15–17